How many HAIRS on a GRIZZLY BEAR? and OTHER BIG NUMBER Questions

?

**For my dad up above, and to my family
and Harry, whom I cherish and love.** Yours, J. K.

A HUGE thank you to:
David Meanwell, Bear Conservation; Jennapher Teunissen van Manen, International
Association for Bear Research and Management; and grizzly bear hair-counter
Savannah Rogers, Bioinformatics and Computational Biology, University of Idaho.

A Raspberry Book
Editorial: Kathryn Jewitt
Art direction & cover design: Sidonie Beresford-Browne
Design: Dorie Morton
Consultant: Dr Mike Goldsmith

KINGFISHER
LONDON & NEW YORK

First published 2021 in the United States by Kingfisher,
120 Broadway, New York, NY 10271
Kingfisher is an imprint of Macmillan Children's Books, London
All rights reserved

ISBN 978-0-7534-7726-7

Library of Congress Cataloging-in-Publication data has been applied for.

Kingfisher books are available for special promotions and premiums.
For details contact:
Special Markets Department, Macmillan,
120 Broadway, New York, NY 10271

For more information please visit:
www.kingfisherbooks.com

Printed in China
1 3 5 7 9 8 6 4 2
1TR/0421/RV/WKT/128MA

How many HAIRS on a GRIZZLY BEAR? and OTHER BIG NUMBER Questions

By
Tracey Turner

With Some Notes
About Numbers
by Kjartan Poskitt

Illustrated by
Jen Khatun

KINGFISHER
LONDON & NEW YORK

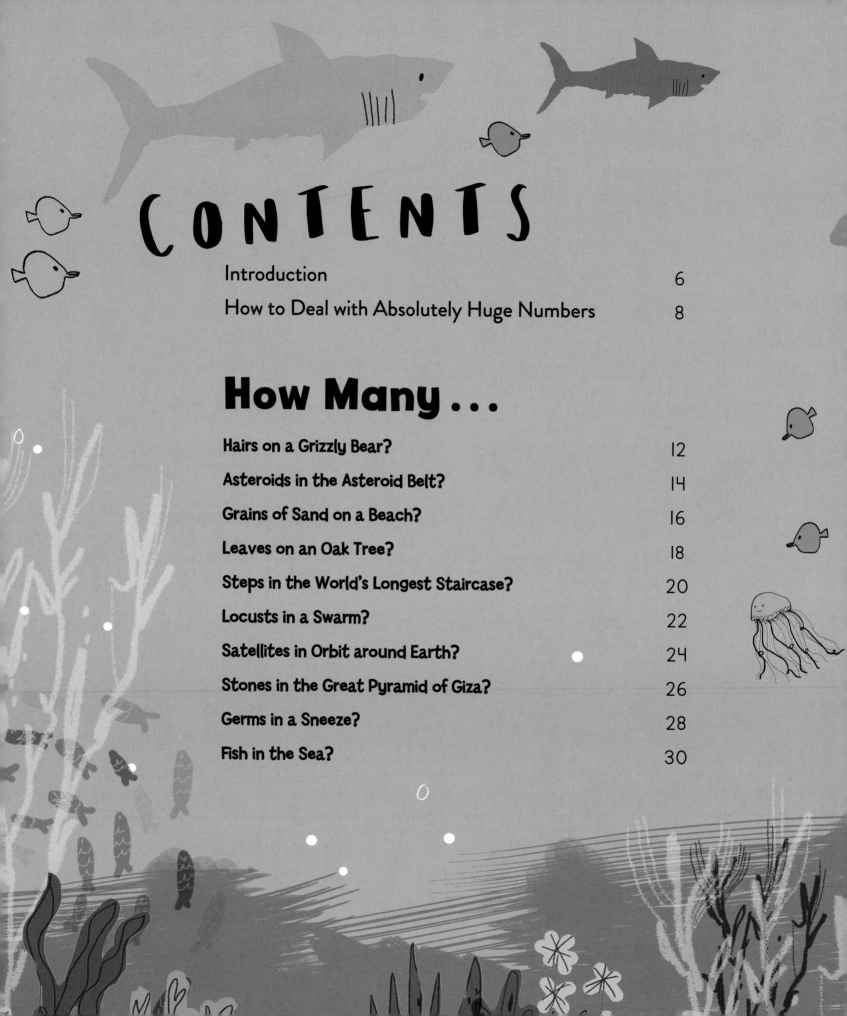

CONTENTS

How Many...

Introduction

Have you ever wondered . . .

. . . how many stars there are in the night sky?

Or how many leaves there are on an oak tree?

Or even how many hairs there are on a grizzly bear?

Well, help is at hand, because we're about to find out.
On the way, we'll . . .

. . . take a close look at snot

. . . go whizzing around the Sun in the asteroid belt

. . . pet the world's furriest animal

. . . climb a staircase to the top of a mountain

. . . and meet an asteroid called Yeti.

As if all that weren't enough, you'll discover a very large number of mind-boggling facts. Find out about farting gorillas, what goes on inside blood cells, and why you should ALWAYS close the toilet lid before you flush.

There are obviously a lot of hairs on a large bear, stars in our galaxy, and all the other things in this book. But if big numbers worry you, **DON'T BE SCARED!** Numbers can tell us some interesting and amazing things—think of them as your friends. But if you're still a little bothered by the thought of them, Kjartan Poskitt, author of Murderous Math and all-round genius, is here to help you get your head around big numbers on the next page.

Some of the questions in this book have exact answers—we know the number of steps in the world's longest staircase, for example. Others have exact answers, but we're never going to be able to find them out for certain—like the number of fish in the sea or stars in our galaxy. And for some, we need to figure out what the question means before we can answer it—before we start counting asteroids in the asteroid belt, we need to ask what is an asteroid, and how big does it have to be before we include it?

Anyway, before we start counting anything, let's turn the page to find out how amazing big numbers are and why you don't need to be afraid of them.

How to deal with ABSOLUTELY HUGE NUMBERS

Take a look at this:

100000000000000

It doesn't tell you much, does it? You could make up a silly name for it, like a zillion or a squillion (no, these are not real number names!), but what is it really?

The first thing to do is divide the zeros up into groups of three, starting on the right:

10,000,000,000,000

This makes the zeros easier to count. Here we've got 13 of them, and we can quickly write this number as 10^{13}. Why? Because 10^{13} tells us to multiply thirteen groups of 10 together. Try it—it works!

So what do we call it? Each group of three digits has a different name. It works like this:

10,000,000,000,000

Trillions (Billions (Millions (Thousands (Hundreds, Tens, and Ones)

Our one with 13 zeros after it is actually ten trillion! (That's roughly the number of kilometers in a light-year—handy to know for when you're traveling through space.)

If your digits are all different, such as 76603124895, you get a whole mixture of names. What do you think this one is called? Let's see . . .

76,603,124,895

Billions (Millions (Thousands (Hundreds, Tens, and Ones)

The number **76,603,124,895** isn't big enough to have any **trillions,** but it has **billions, millions, thousands,** and finally the **hundreds, tens,** and **ones.** Here comes the fun part, because we can now read out the number . . .

> Seventy six billion,
> six hundred and three million,
> one hundred and twenty-four thousand,
> eight hundred and ninety-five.

Even bigger numbers

When you see *bi, tri, quad,* and *quint* in front of words, they mean two, three, four, and five. That's why there are three wheels on a tricycle and four babies in quadruplets.

1,000	We start out with three zeros to make a **thousand.**
1,000,000	One more set of three zeros makes a **million.**
1,000,000,000	Two more sets make a **billion.**
1,000,000,000,000	Three more sets make a **trillion.**
1,000,000,000,000,000	Four more sets make a **quadrillion.**
1,000,000,000,000,000,000 . . .	Five more sets make a **quintillion.**

After that it's **sextillion, septillion, octillion, nonillion, decillion** . . .

The Fancy Way to Write Big Numbers

It's much easier to write the number **40,000,000,000,000** as 4×10^{13}. This is the "scientific notation" that scientists use, and the most important part is that little number **13**. This is the power of ten, which tells you whether the number will be small, big, or amazingly huge. Suppose the number was **47,200,000,000,000**. It should be written like this: 4.72×10^{13}

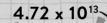

4.72×10^{13}

Leading digit   **Power of 10**

If you see a number such as 5.21×10^6, how do you write it out in full? The little **6** tells you to multiply the **5.21** by **1,000,000.** You can do this by moving the digits six places to the left. The decimal point stays in the same place and you fill in the gaps with zeros.

$5.21 \times 10^6 = 5210000.0 = 5,210,000$

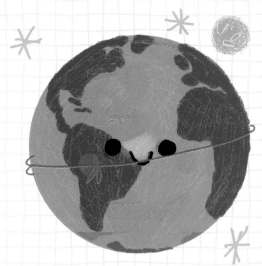

That depends on what you need your huge number for. For instance, how far is it around the equator? One answer is 25,000 miles. This would be useful if you were going to fly around the world and you needed to figure out how long it might take you. It's easy to write down and remember.

Now let's suppose you wanted to tie a piece of string around Earth. You'd find 25,000 miles was too long. A more accurate answer is 24,901 miles.

But people don't usually tie strings around the equator, so the rough distance 25,000 (or 2.5×10^4) miles is close enough. In fact, for most huge numbers, we just need a general idea of size. When you see a number ending in a lot of zeros, it's probably been rounded off to make things simple.

How Close Are Our Answers?

We could work out some big numbers exactly if we really wanted to—for example, the number of stones in the Great Pyramid, because they are big and chunky and aren't going anywhere. But it would mean taking the entire Great Pyramid apart, so we'd better not. Instead we've used an Egyptologist's estimate.

When we work out the number of hairs on a grizzly bear, we know how many hairs are in a square inch because of our bear expert friends, but we don't know exactly how big the bear is, and he might have a good old scratching session and pull a few hairs out. But none of that matters. If we make some intelligent estimates, we'll get a reasonable answer.

Hairs on a grizzly bear accuracy

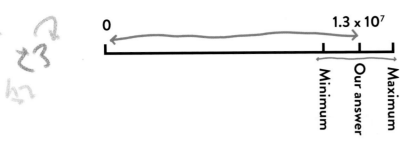

0   1.3 x 10⁷

Minimum Our answer Maximum

Here the green line indicates the size of the answer, and the red line shows our "margin of error." The shorter the red line, the more accurate our answer is.

Grains of sand on a beach accuracy

When we look at the grains of sand on a beach, the beach could be any size. Although we worked out the answer was about 5.94 quadrillion, the 5.94 could be 9 or more, or even 1 or less.

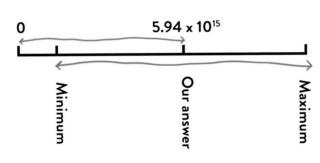

0   5.94 x 10¹⁵

Minimum   Our answer   Maximum

This might not look very accurate, but we do know that we're talking quadrillions here, and that's enough grains of sand for anybody! We could just say "a few quadrillion."

Now that we know what **billions, trillions,** and **quadrillions** are, let's go find some!

How Many HAiRS on a GRiZZLY BEAR?

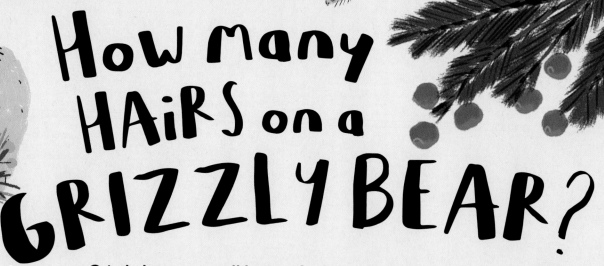

Grizzly bears are well known for being hairy, as well as very large and frightening. But just how hairy are they?

Surprisingly, we know how many hairs a grizzly bear has per square inch (sq. in.), because someone has counted! Research at the University of Idaho has given us an exact number for a grizzly wearing its winter coat. We are making an estimate for the size of our bear, though.

Grizzly bears are a type of brown bear, and some have fur tipped with white or gray. Graying hair can be called "grizzled," and that's how grizzly bears got their name.

TO WORK IT OUT

Hairs in 1 sq. in. of a grizzly's fur: 2,652
Grizzly bear's surface area: 5,000 sq. in.
Multiply 2,652 hairs x 5,000 sq. in. . . .

There are about **13,260,000**
(13.26 MILLION) hairs on a grizzly bear!
No wonder they keep warm in Alaskan winters.

Grizzlies are BIG bears—they can be almost 10 ft. (3 m) tall if they stand on their hind legs. But to make themselves look even bigger and scarier, grizzlies can bristle their many hairs to make them stand on end.

YUM!

There isn't much a grizzly bear won't eat. Berries, fruit, grasses, seeds, honey, worms, small mammals, young elk and bison . . . you name it, they're happy to dig in. They are partial to moths, and a grizzly can eat 40,000 of them in one day.

Grizzlies aren't all that hairy compared with some other animals, especially the sea otter, which has the densest fur in the world. Other sea mammals have a layer of blubber to keep them warm, but not sea otters. They keep warm by being very, very furry, with around 900,000 hairs per square inch on average.

How many hairs do you have compared with a grizzly bear? You probably have around 115,000 individual hairs on your head, and around 5 million hairs covering your whole body. Grizzlies are around two and a half times hairier. Their hairs are much longer, and they have a very curly undercoat, which gives them their super-furry look.

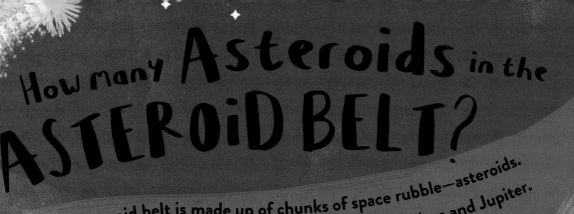

How many Asteroids in the ASTEROID BELT?

The asteroid belt is made up of chunks of space rubble—asteroids. They whiz around the Sun between the orbits of Mars and Jupiter. But what are they, and how many are there?

Asteroids are the leftover pieces of rock and metal from when the planets in our solar system formed, around 4.6 billion years ago. In addition to the ones in the asteroid belt, there are other asteroids in the solar system.

The biggest asteroid in the asteroid belt is a dwarf planet called Ceres, with a diameter of 590 mi. (950 km). That's about the same as the length (or width) of France. Vesta is the only other dwarf planet in the asteroid belt.

To qualify as an asteroid, an object has to be bigger than 0.6 mi. (1 km) across. There are trillions of smaller bits and pieces, all the way down to dust grains, but these are called meteoroids. Counting just asteroids, it's still very difficult to say how many there are for sure.

The asteroid belt is a vast disk shape. It's so big that even though there are millions of asteroids, there's so much space between them that a spacecraft's chances of crashing into one are less than 1 in a billion. So far, 13 spacecraft have entered or traveled through it without bumping into anything (except on purpose, which is what the spacecraft NEAR Shoemaker did in 2001)!

Most asteroids aren't round like planets—they look more like beaten-up potatoes. Some of them have one or two little moons that orbit around them, and some orbit one another, like space rock best friends.

The European Space Agency's Infrared Space Observatory satellite (ISO) estimated that there are between 1.1 MILLION and 1.9 MILLION ASTEROIDS in the main asteroid belt.

Ceres and Vesta are the names of two ancient Roman deities and are very sensible names for asteroids. Others have more unusual names, including James Bond (asteroid number 9007) and Mr. Spock (after a *Star Trek* character). One is even called Yeti.

One of the reasons scientists study asteroids is to figure out when a big one might come hurtling toward Earth! Asteroids big enough to destroy a city strike our planet every few centuries, but so little of Earth has a city on it that there's only a tiny chance of one actually being destroyed.

HOW MANY GRAINS of SAND on a BEACH?

You are just adding the finishing touches to your sandcastle when this question pops into your head. Hang on to your sun hat, because this one has a REALLY big number for an answer.

There are three things we need to do to work it out. 1) Determine how many grains of sand there are in a bucket. 2) Determine how many buckets of sand there are on our beach. 3) Determine how many grains of sand there are on the beach. To start with, count out 100 grains of sand (this seagull is helping) and weigh them.

We just need a rough number of grains of sand, so we're not going to worry about how wet it is and things like that.

TO WORK OUT HOW MANY GRAINS OF SAND PER BUCKET

- **100 grains of sand = 0.0014 ounces (oz.)**
- Our bucket of sand weighs **7.875 lb. = 126 oz.**
- Divide the weight of the bucket of sand by the weight of **100 grains**: **126 ÷ 0.0014 = 90,000**
- Multiply by **100** to get the number of grains per bucket:
- **90,000 x 100 = 9,000,000 (9 million grains per bucket)**

Our beach covers an area of around **550,000 sq. ft.** We know that the sand is about **80 ft.** deep.

TO WORK OUT HOW MANY GRAINS OF SAND ON THE BEACH

- Volume of sand = **550,000 sq. ft.** (area) x **80 ft.** (depth) = **44,000,000 cubic feet**
- Multiply by **60** to make pints: **2,640,000,000**
- Our bucket of sand contains about **4 pints**
  So the beach contains **2,640,000,000 (2.64 billion) pt. ÷ 4 pt. = 660,000,000 (660 million)** buckets of sand.
- Each bucket contains about **9 million grains**.
- **9 million grains of sand x 660 million buckets . . .**

There are (very roughly)

5,940,000,000,000,000—

5 quadrillion, 940 trillion—or 5.94×10^{15}— grains of sand on our beach. No wonder some has gotten in your shorts.

Even though that number is unimaginably huge, and the world has a large number of beaches, there are STILL more stars in the sky than grains of sand on all of Earth's beaches.

The longest beach in the world is Praia do Cassino, in the state of Rio Grande do Sul in Brazil. It stretches for 132 mi. (212 km).

How many LEAVES on an OAK TREE?

Oak trees can grow to 130 ft. (40 m) tall—the height of a 12-story building—and almost as wide. So I hope you're okay with heights.

We don't really need to climb our oak tree. Instead, we can count the leaves on a small branch, measure the length of the branch and how far from the trunk it is, and other bits and pieces, and then use the numbers to make an estimate, using a brainy computer and some clever math.

They estimated that the oak tree had **227,721 LEAVES.**

In fact, the University of Washington did exactly that, using a mature common oak tree that looked a little bit like this one. It works because each branch on the tree is like a small version of the tree itself, and each branch is made up of even smaller versions.

Oak trees can live for more than a thousand years, but the oldest trees in the world are quaking aspen trees in Utah. The trees are a colony, known as Pando, and share an underground root system and a single ancestor estimated to be 80,000 years old. The oldest individual tree is just a baby by comparison—it's a Great Basin bristlecone pine that lives in California and is roughly 5,060 years old.

By the way, never have a picnic under an oak tree. In hot, dry weather they sometimes shed whole branches to reduce the amount of water they need. Some other trees do this too, but oak branches are especially big and heavy—and often high up.

Our oak tree's leaves are a sensible size, but some trees go TOO FAR. A palm tree called *Raphia regalis* has leaves that can measure more than **80 ft. (25 m) long** and **10 ft. (3 m) wide**—the biggest in the world. We'd need about **57,600 oak leaves** to make one of those enormous leaves, about one-third of all the leaves on our tree. (Look at page 48 to see how we worked this out.)

How MANY STEPS in the world's longest STAIRCASE?

The world's longest staircase isn't in a building—it's called the Niesen Treppenlauf, and it runs up the side of a 7,753 ft. (2,363 m) tall mountain called the Niesen in Switzerland. A train runs up the mountain on very steep tracks, and next to the tracks is our staircase.

The steps are used to get to the railroad for repairs or in an emergency, and the staircase isn't open to the public. But once a year there's a race up the Niesen Treppenlauf for very tough, super-fit competitors. Up to 500 people start the race, but if someone doesn't complete the first half within an hour, they're disqualified. The winning time is usually about one hour in total, but most runners take much longer than that.

There are 11,674 STEPS on the NIESEN TREPPENLAUF. At least you get a good view when you make it to the top.

Count the number of steps in the staircase in your house, or between floors in your apartment building or your school, then divide the number into 11,674. How many times would you need to climb your stairs to have the same experience as the runners?

The steps in the Niesen Treppenlauf are almost certain to be a lot steeper than your staircase. Steepness, or gradient, is usually shown as a percentage—you divide the distance traveled up in a straight line by the distance traveled horizontally. The gradient of this triangle is 15 divided by 3 = 5, or 500% as a percentage.

15 ft.

3 ft.

GO TEAM!

YAY!

We love you!

How many LOCUSTS in a SWARM?

NOM!

Locusts have a terrible but well-deserved reputation for zooming around and eating everything in sight. How many of the little munchers are there in a swarm?

YUM!

Locusts are a kind of grasshopper, and sometimes they behave like other grasshoppers—hopping around in a quiet kind of way. But they have an unusual and terrifying difference. In certain circumstances—usually when they become overcrowded, often in damp weather—they swarm. They change color and body shape, become very friendly with one another, and—crucially— very HUNGRY for green plants.

MUNCH!!

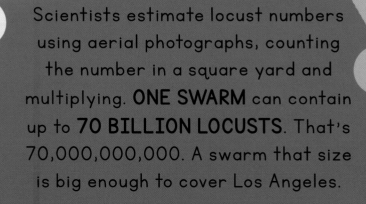

Scientists estimate locust numbers using aerial photographs, counting the number in a square yard and multiplying. **ONE SWARM** can contain up to **70 BILLION LOCUSTS**. That's 70,000,000,000. A swarm that size is big enough to cover Los Angeles.

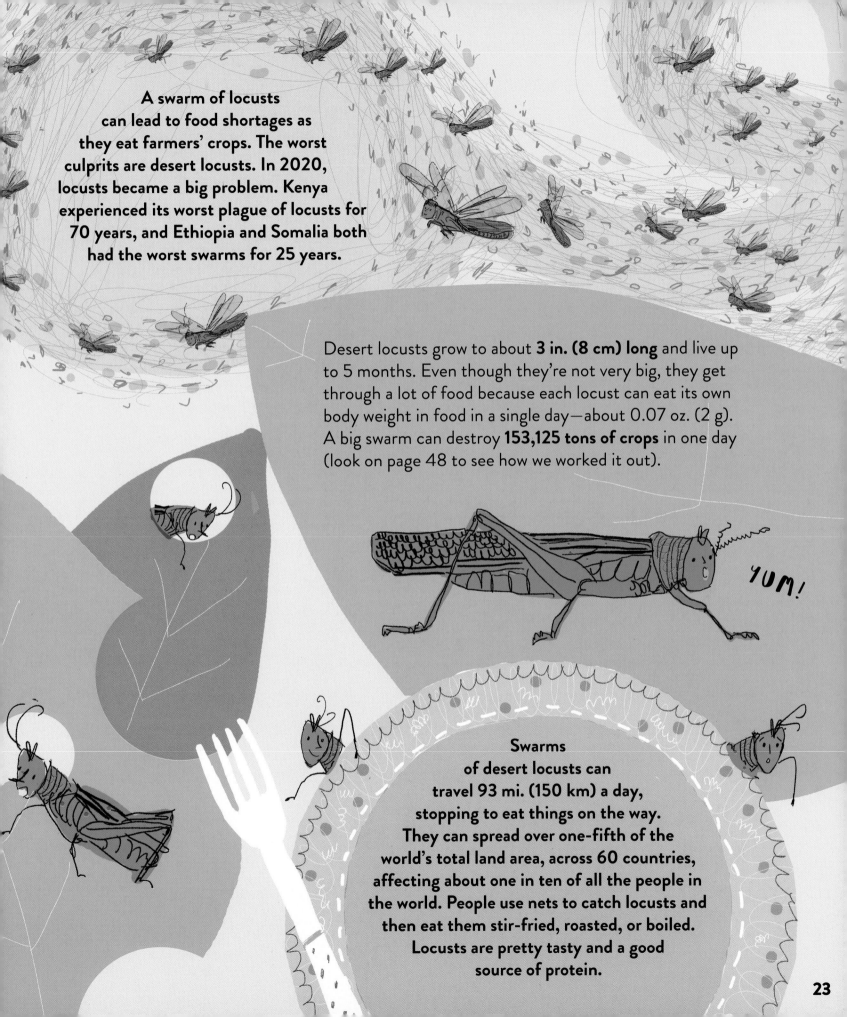

A swarm of locusts can lead to food shortages as they eat farmers' crops. The worst culprits are desert locusts. In 2020, locusts became a big problem. Kenya experienced its worst plague of locusts for 70 years, and Ethiopia and Somalia both had the worst swarms for 25 years.

Desert locusts grow to about **3 in. (8 cm) long** and live up to 5 months. Even though they're not very big, they get through a lot of food because each locust can eat its own body weight in food in a single day—about 0.07 oz. (2 g). A big swarm can destroy **153,125 tons of crops** in one day (look on page 48 to see how we worked it out).

YUM!

Swarms of desert locusts can travel 93 mi. (150 km) a day, stopping to eat things on the way. They can spread over one-fifth of the world's total land area, across 60 countries, affecting about one in ten of all the people in the world. People use nets to catch locusts and then eat them stir-fried, roasted, or boiled. Locusts are pretty tasty and a good source of protein.

23

How MANY SATELLITES in Orbit Around EARTH?

It's not only stars that twinkle in the night sky—so do satellites. How many are there, and what are they up to?

The very first satellite—and the first human-made object in space—was called Sputnik 1 (*sputnik* is Russian for "traveling companion"). It was sent into orbit by the Soviet Union in 1957 and stayed there for three months. For the first few weeks, until its batteries ran out, it sent out radio signals, heard as beeps on radio receivers on Earth.

Satellites are objects that orbit a planet. So the Moon is a satellite of Earth. There are many, many more human-made ones.

Today objects in orbit around Earth include the International Space Station (which is the size of a football field) and the Hubble Space Telescope, as well as flakes of paint, nuts and bolts, and other space junk. There are more than 34,000 objects bigger than 4 in. (10 cm) circling our planet.

Scientists estimate there are about **5,640 SATELLITES IN ORBIT** around Earth. Around 2,800 are still functioning.

The International Space Station is a space science lab where astronauts carry out zero-gravity experiments. Other satellites are there to help with navigation and communication, to take pictures of our solar system and deep space, and to monitor the weather.

There are plans for thousands more satellites to be launched, so the number in orbit could easily double or triple in the near future. When they've reached the end of their working lives, old satellites can either be sent farther away from Earth—into a "graveyard orbit"—or slowed down so that they return to Earth, burning up in the atmosphere as they fall.

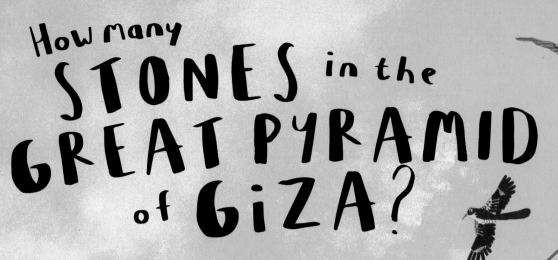

The Great Pyramid of Giza in Egypt is still standing 4,500 years after it was first built. How many stones did it take to build this great big structure?

The pyramid is one of the Seven Wonders of the World. It's the oldest and also the only one that still exists. When the ancient Romans visited the pyramid, it was already an ancient tourist attraction, at two thousand years old!

755 ft. (230 m)

The Great Pyramid is the biggest of all the Egyptian pyramids, and it is absolutely enormous. It was the world's tallest building for more than 3,800 years, until Lincoln Cathedral in England was built in the 1300s.

The outside of the pyramid used to be covered with limestone blocks, polished so that the pyramid shone in the sun. By the 1800s, most of them had been removed and used elsewhere, along with the stones at the very top.

It's impossible to know the exact number of stones in the pyramid without taking it apart and upsetting everyone, but in the 1880s an archaeologist named William Matthew Flinders Petrie made a very good guess. He worked out the pyramid's volume, then subtracted an estimate for the mound of earth and passageways inside it. Then he worked out the average volume of a stone to arrive at his number.

The pyramids of ancient Egypt were built as tombs. The Great Pyramid was the tomb of the pharaoh (or king) Khufu. His dead body was mummified— preserved and bandaged—and placed inside the pyramid along with all the things he would need in the afterlife: food, clothes, jewelry, weapons, even a great wooden ship. The ancient Egyptians thought people would need some of their insides in the afterlife as well, so they put them in jars—but not their brains, which they didn't think were important.

There are roughly **2.3 MILLION (2,300,000) HUGE STONES IN THE GREAT PYRAMID**. Petrie's estimate is still accepted today.

Around **6 million tons of limestone**, **8,800 tons of granite**—brought from 500 mi. (800 km away)—and **550,000 tons of mortar** were used to build the pyramid.

How many GERMS in a SNEEZE?

All kinds of nasty infections can be caught from a sneeze, so this is a vital—and horrifying—thing to know.

Germs are tiny organisms that cause disease. They include bacteria and viruses, which can cause colds and other diseases. They're invisible unless you look at them through a microscope. There are other kinds of germs too.

SNIFF

AA...

A sneeze releases a fine mist of saliva (spit) and mucus (snot). Seen in slow motion, it is surprisingly disgusting. The spit and snot droplets can spread as far as **33 ft. (10 m)** from an unguarded sneeze.

Scientists at the University of Bristol, in England, have put a lot of time and effort into finding out the horrors that lurk in an average sneeze of someone with a cold:

There are around **100,000 GERMS** per average sneeze.

Whether you catch something from a sneezing person depends on your immune system. You might be immune to some infections and cheerfully breathe in infected snot without catching them. Or your immune system might be unable to fight off infections because you already have a different disease or are taking certain medicines—then, only a tiny number of germs would give you the infection.

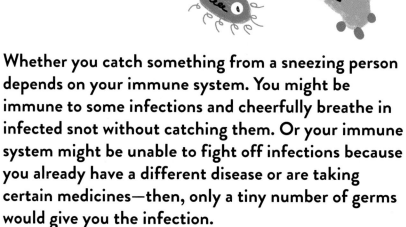

The worst time for spreading germs is right after sneezing, so don't stand around saying bless you and inhaling snot at the same time. If you sneeze, cover your mouth and nose and use a tissue to catch all the droplets. Then throw the tissue away.

CHOO!!

Smaller droplets can hang around suspended in the air for weeks, though usually it's just a few minutes. Bigger ones quickly land on the floor or surrounding objects, ready for someone to touch. So make sure you wash your hands regularly and thoroughly, because that will get rid of any germs.

While we're on the subject of germs, always close the toilet lid before you flush! If you don't, an invisible 3 ft. (1 m) high germ-laden spray is released into the bathroom, quite possibly landing on your toothbrush.

HOW many FiSh in the SEA?

Planet Earth is mostly sea, and it is full of fish, so the answer is obviously going to be a lot. But how many fish are there, and how on earth can we work it out?

Counting fish is hard—the ocean is wide and deep, fish are good at hiding, and they have a habit of swimming around. It's also important, because we need to find out as much as we can in order to protect our oceans and the animals that live in them.

Scientists try to count fish using different methods, depending on where the fish live. They might use trawlers, drones, spotter planes, undersea robots, or sound waves. A lot of the counting is done by artificial intelligence systems—which must be a relief to the scientists. These studies can tell us about particular kinds of fish and other animals, and whether their numbers are rising or falling. They can't really tell us how many fish there are in the sea altogether, though.

It's a little easier to count how many fish have been caught, because fisheries around the world keep records. One study came to a (very rough) conclusion . . .

The **NUMBER OF FISH CAUGHT IN THE SEA PER YEAR** is somewhere between about **1 AND 3 TRILLION** (a trillion is one million times a million, or 1,000,000,000,000, or 10^{12}). That's just the ones that are caught!

New fish species are discovered all the time. Scientists think that roughly 22,000 different kinds of fish have been discovered so far, and those fish can be very different from one another. The smallest fish, for example, is the pygmy goby, which grows to about 0.5 in. (12 mm) long. The largest fish is the whale shark, which can grow more than 800 times bigger than the goby—up to 33 ft. (10 m) long.

There are some questions no one can answer, even roughly, despite the fact that there is an exact answer.

How many RAINDROPS in a CLOUD?

There are many different types of clouds, and not all of them bring rain—some are quite happy just to float around. What are they made of, what makes them rain, and how many raindrops are waiting to fall?

Clouds are made up of tiny droplets of water or ice that float in the air, each formed around a tiny particle, which might be a minuscule speck of dust or salt from the sea. The water droplets don't become raindrops and fall unless they're heavy enough.

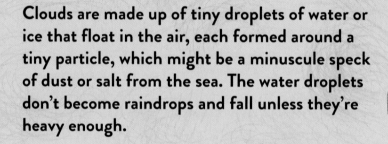

Different types of clouds have different amounts of water in them. Our **cloud has roughly 0.0005 oz. of water per cubic foot (cu. ft.)**, and its **volume is 256 million cu. ft.**. So the **cloud weighs 128,000 oz.**, or **4 tons** (look on page 48 to see how we worked this out).

Although the cloud is floating around in the sky, looking white and fluffy and not raining, it **weighs as much an adult African elephant**. All that weight is very spread out, though, and rising warm air pushes it up, so the cloud stays in the air instead of plummeting to the ground and crushing things.

Clouds form rain when they cool and water vapor in the cloud condenses onto the tiny water droplets.

The droplets grow and join together. They become too heavy to float in the air, so they fall as rain. Single clouds don't usually rain all on their own—they get together with other clouds, and rain falls from a clouded sky, which looks gray because of the way the light bounces off the bigger droplets.

If the droplets weigh about 0.004 oz., they fall slowly as drizzle. Our cloud has ganged up with some other big clouds, so it's going to form large raindrops that weigh 0.128 oz. and absolutely pelt down.

 ## TO WORK IT OUT

Our cloud contains 4 tons of water. Half of it is going to keep floating around as water vapor, so 2 tons of water are going to become raindrops.
1 ton = 32,000 oz., so we'll get **64,000 oz. of rain.**
Our **raindrops weigh 0.128 oz.** each.
Divide 64,000 by 0.128 . . .

Our cloud is just about to MAKE AND DROP 500 THOUSAND (500,000) RAINDROPS. I hope you have an umbrella.

How many CELLS in the HUMAN BODY?

Cells are very tiny indeed compared with the size of a human being. So get ready for a VERY big number.

All living things are made up of cells. In the human body there are more than 200 different kinds—skin cells, blood cells, cells that make up your bones and muscle, cells that change food into energy, cells that send and receive information in your brain, and all kinds of others. They can be long and thin, like nerve cells, or disk shaped with a dimple in the middle, like red blood cells.

Counting cells might sound pretty straightforward, but because cells aren't all the same size or weight, and because they aren't spread out in a regular way inside our bodies, it's a difficult question to answer.

Luckily, we don't have to try to work this out, because a group of scientists has done all the hard work for us. They looked at each type of cell in all the organs and other stuff in the average adult human body, from the cartilage in the average nose to the nail on the average toe, and then they added everything up . . .

There are **37.2 TRILLION** (that's 37,200,000,000,000, or 3.72×10^{13}) **CELLS** in the **HUMAN BODY**.

cell nucleus

There is a lot going on inside every one of those **37.2 trillion cells**. Structures called organelles do particular jobs—making or storing chemicals, breaking down dead stuff—and tubes carry material around inside the cell. A cell's nucleus is its control center, telling the cell what to do and when to copy itself. All of this is going on inside cells that are so tiny you could fit thousands of them on the head of a pin.

OI!!

Not all cells are teeny tiny: birds' eggs are cells. The biggest animal cell in the world is an ostrich egg!

How many BOOKS in the World's BIGGEST Library?

The world's biggest library is the Library of Congress in Washington, DC. You would have a LOT of choice if you went to visit. Just how many books does it contain?

The United States Congress, the lawmaking branch of the federal government, meets in the Capitol Building on Capitol Hill in Washington, DC. The Library of Congress was inside the Capitol Building at first, but now the library is spread across three separate buildings.

The number of books is changing all the time, as more books are added. So we can only give a rough estimate—unless we're talking about a particular day.

OF MICE AND MEN

The **LIBRARY OF CONGRESS CONTAINS** about **25 MILLION (25,000,000)** cataloged **BOOKS**. But if you include everything the library contains, there are more than 170 million items.

If you read **10 books a week** at the Library of Congress, you'd need to **live for almost 48,000 years before you'd looked at every book!** (To see how we worked this out, look on page 48.)

These are some of the things the library contains besides books (the numbers are approximate):

5,600,000 ...... maps
8,100,000 ...... pieces of sheet music
4,200,000 ..... recordings
14,800,000 ..... photographs
110,000 .... posters
690,000 .... prints and drawings

Libraries have been around for at least 2,600 years. The oldest one discovered belonged to Ashurbanipal, King of Assyria, who ruled in the 600s BC from his palace in Nineveh, now in Iraq.

In 1789, the first US president, George Washington, borrowed *The Law of Nations* from the New York Society Library and never returned it! In 2010, staff at Washington's home, now a museum, gave the library a copy of the book (though not the same one)—221 years late.

People also read a lot online. There are more than **1.78 billion (1,780,000,000) websites,** and more than **5.46 billion (5,460,000,000) web pages** to choose from on the Internet.

How many GORILLAS in the JUNGLE?

They're our closest relatives after chimpanzees and bonobos, so we really should take an interest in how they're doing. How many of our beautiful, furry cousins are there in the wild?

Gorillas live in the jungle of central and western Africa. It's very hard to find out how many there are because they live in dense and remote forests, and they flatly refuse to fill out census forms. But scientists and forest rangers track and record them, so we can take a rough guess . . .

There are somewhere between about **100,000 AND 360,000 GORILLAS** in the **JUNGLE**. There are also some in zoos, which are a lot easier to count, for obvious reasons: about **4,000**.

Gorillas make different hoots, grunts, and growly sounds to communicate with each other. Sometimes they beat their chests with their fists—which makes a sound somewhat like a wooden xylophone—to warn of danger, to show that they're in the mood for a fight, or just to show off.

If we say the gorillas are 5 ft. tall on average, and ask them to lie down in a long line on the world's longest bridge, which is the **102.4 mi. long Danyang-Kunshang Grand Bridge in China**, they'd reach to the end and then some—even near the lower estimate of gorillas in the jungle. (Look on page 48 to see how we worked this out.)

They might look scary, but generally gorillas are pretty peaceful, laid-back creatures. To maintain their size, eating takes up a lot of a gorilla's time. They're mainly vegetarian, chomping away at fruit, roots, and bark, with the occasional worm or insect. All that fiber makes them some of the world's gassiest animals.

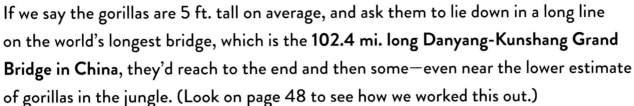

PARP!
Toot!

Sadly, all gorillas are endangered, like the other great apes—chimpanzees, bonobos, and orangutans. They're at risk from disease, from forests being cleared, and because they're hunted for food or as pets. A lot of good work is being done to protect them and to increase the number of gorillas in the jungle.

How many STARS in the MILKY WAY?

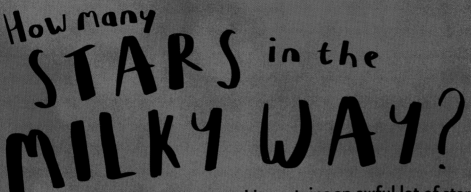

The Milky Way is our galaxy, and it contains an awful lot of stars. How many are there, and how do we count them?

If it's a really clear moonless night and you are far away from artificial lights, you'll be able to make out the Milky Way as a thick band of stars, like a white path in the night sky. We can also see thousands of nearby stars just using our eyes, and thousands more with a telescope.

Our galaxy is so enormous that light, which zips along at about 186,000 mi. (300,000 km) every second, takes 105,700 years to travel across it.

To answer the question, scientists first have to estimate the mass of the Milky Way—there are smaller galaxies in orbit around ours, and scientists use their movements to work it out. Then they have to work out how much of that mass is stars, and not dust or gas. Finally, they have to estimate the mass of an average star. None of these things is known exactly, so scientists give a range.

The Milky Way is a spiral galaxy (the best shape for a galaxy, obviously), but there are other kinds too, including elliptical and irregular. Planet Earth is about here.

There are between 100 BILLION AND 400 BILLION STARS in the MILKY WAY!

We don't know how big the whole universe is, but we do know a bit about the part of it that we can see with super telescopes (the "observable universe"). Roughly, that's the volume of space within around 13.8 billion light-years (a light-year is the distance light travels in a year), because any light from farther away hasn't had time to reach us since the universe began, 13.8 billion years ago. The observable universe probably contains at least 2 trillion galaxies.

Scientists have worked out the number of STARS in the OBSERVABLE UNIVERSE as 100 SEXTILLION, or 100,000,000,000,000,000,000,000 (10^{23}), the biggest number in this book. But there could easily be three times that many!

HOW MANY PEOPLE in the WORLD?

Since human beings first evolved many thousands of years ago, we've completely taken over the planet. Just how many of us are there now?

This number is growing all the time, so we can only give a rough estimate for the number of people in the world, and we can't really know exactly how many of us there are. There aren't records for every single person in the world (and some of us might be hiding). At the moment . . .

There are roughly **7.8 BILLION** (7 billion, 8 hundred million, or 7,800,000,000) **PEOPLE** in the world today.

The estimate back in 1970 was 3.7 billion people. By 2030, it's expected to be more than 8 billion.

Countries with Highest Populations

CHINA: more than 1.4 billion
INDIA: more than 1.3 billion—and expected to overtake China by 2030
UNITED STATES: 331 million
INDONESIA: 274 million
PAKISTAN: 221 million

Countries with Lowest Populations

If you count Vatican City in Rome, Italy, as a country, its population is even lower than Tuvalu, at around 800 people.

TUVALU: 11,600
NAURU: 12,800
PALAU: 20,000
SAN MARINO: 28,500
MONACO: 32,200

Most of us (roughly six out of every ten people in the world) live on the continent of Asia. Roughly two out of every ten people live in an African country, and the rest (the remaining two out of every ten people) live in the rest of the world—in Europe, Australia and the South Pacific, and North and South America.

The only continent where no one lives permanently is Antarctica, which is so cold that even penguins have a hard time.

Brrr!

All of those people speak thousands of languages —more than 6,500 different ones. But half of the people in the world speak one of just 23 languages. The top five most widely spoken are Mandarin Chinese, English, Spanish, Hindi, and Bengali.

From BIG to ENORMOUS

It's time to have a look at all our lovely numbers in order of size. Gosh, some of them are really big, aren't they?

5,640 SATELLITES IN ORBIT AROUND EARTH.
Or if you want to use fancy scientific notation, 5.64×10^3 satellites spinning through space. But we have lots of bigger numbers . . .

11,674 STEPS ON THE WORLD'S LONGEST STAIRCASE.
Or 1.1674×10^4. This is an absolutely astonishing number if you happen to be climbing them.

500,000 RAINDROPS IN A CLOUD.
That's 5×10^5. And our cloud isn't even very big. The next number is chunkier still . . .

1,900,000 ASTEROIDS IN THE ASTEROID BELT.
There are between 1.1 and 1.9 million, or 1.9×10^6, asteroids up there.

2,300,000 STONES IN THE GREAT PYRAMID.
The stones are pretty hefty, and there are 2.3 million, or 2.3×10^6, of them. Now we're moving into the **supersize** category . . .

13,260,000 HAIRS ON A GRIZZLY BEAR.
Our grizzly bear has 13.26 million, or 1.326×10^7, hairs (give or take a few).

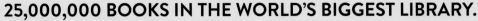

25,000,000 BOOKS IN THE WORLD'S BIGGEST LIBRARY.

The Library of Congress contains roughly 25 million, or 2.5×10^7, books. Going up a level to **gigantic** . . .

7,800,000,000 PEOPLE IN THE WORLD.

There are about 7.8 billion, or 7.8×10^9, of us. The next one's **colossal** . . .

70,000,000,000 LOCUSTS IN A SWARM.

That's 70 billion, or 7×10^{10}, hungry insects. Add yet another 0 and we're in **monumentally huge** territory . . .

400,000,000,000 STARS IN THE MILKY WAY.

Our galaxy contains between 100 billion and 400 billion, or 4×10^{11}, stars. Get ready for an **absolutely immense** number . . .

37,200,000,000,000 CELLS IN THE HUMAN BODY.

Your body is made up of about 37.2 trillion, or 3.72×10^{13}, cells. And now for a **mind-blowingly enormous** number . . .

5,940,000,000,000,000 GRAINS OF SAND ON OUR BEACH.

Our little beach contains 5 quadrillion, 940 trillion grains of sand— or 5.94×10^{15}. But there's still one last number, which just might make your head explode with its **gigantically huge vastness** . . .

100,000,000,000,000,000,000,000 STARS IN THE OBSERVABLE UNIVERSE.

The biggest number we've seen in this book is an estimate of the number of stars in the part of the universe that we could see with a powerful enough telescope. It's the same as 100 sextillion, or 10^{23}.

Index

TO WORK IT OUT

Page 19 Oak Leaves:
The leaves are leaf-shaped, but we're pretending they're rectangles. If we said an oak tree leaf measures 2 in. long by 1 in. wide, **how many would we need to make one *Raphia regalis* leaf?**
Rough area of oak leaf = 2 x 1 in. = 2 in.
Rough area of *Raphia regalis* leaf = 80 ft. x 10. ft = 800 sq. ft. (115,200 sq. in.)
Divide the area of the big leaf by the small one: 115,200 divided by 2 = 57,600

Page 28 Locusts:
One locust weighs 0.07 oz. and can eat its own body weight in a day. So:
0.07 oz. x 70,000,000,000 locusts = 4,900,000,000 (4.9 billion) oz. = 153,125 tons

Page 32 Cloud:
To find the volume of the cloud (which is cloud-shaped, but we're saying it's a cuboid to work this out):
1,000 ft. long x 1,000 ft. wide x 256 ft. tall = 256,000,000 or 256 million cu. ft.
If each cubic foot contains 0.0005 oz. of water, that's 256,000,000 x 0.0005 = 128,000 oz., or 4 tons.

Page 36 Books in the Library of Congress:
There are 52 weeks in a year, and you read 10 books per week: 52 x 10 = 520.
Now we divide all the books in the library by the number of books you read in one year:
24,863,177 divided by 520 = 47,814 (rounded up to the nearest whole number)

Page 39 Gorillas on a Bridge:
Average gorilla height (we're saying): 5 ft.
All gorillas lying down in a line:
5 x 110,000 (near the lower estimate of gorilla numbers) = 550,000 ft.
Danyang-Kunshang Grand Bridge is 102.4 mi. long, which is 540,672 ft.